FIDDLESTICKS

THE "CLEAN"
SWEAR WORD
COLORING BOOK

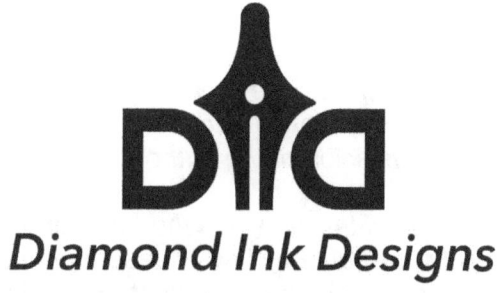

Diamond Ink Designs

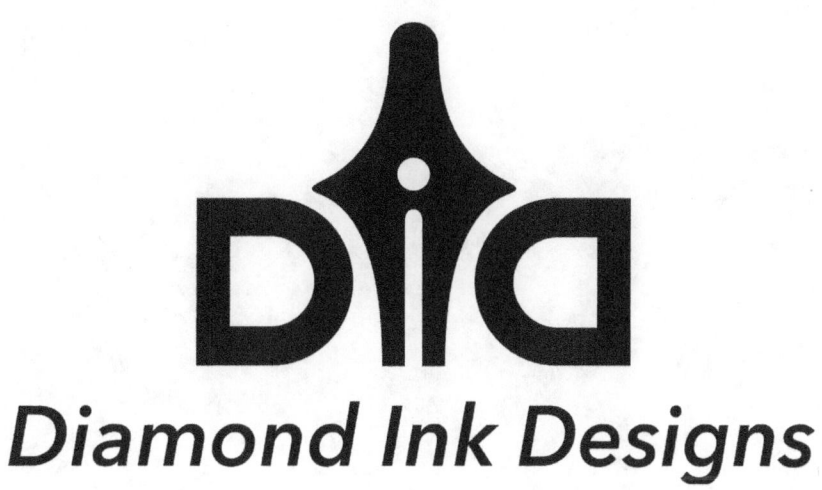

Diamond Ink Designs

VIP CLUB

Please take this opportunity to join our VIP CLUB.

Go To: **http://eepurl.com/bQPz5f**

By joining you will receive a bonus high quality printable coloring page. You will also be entered into future giveaways such as; adult coloring books, professional grade coloring pencils, as well as other printable free coloring pages.

We hope you freaking love our coloring book you turd. Now you can let off some flippin' steam without feeling like you are going straight to H.E. Double Hockey Sticks. Have a heck of a good time coloring.

-Diamond Ink Designs

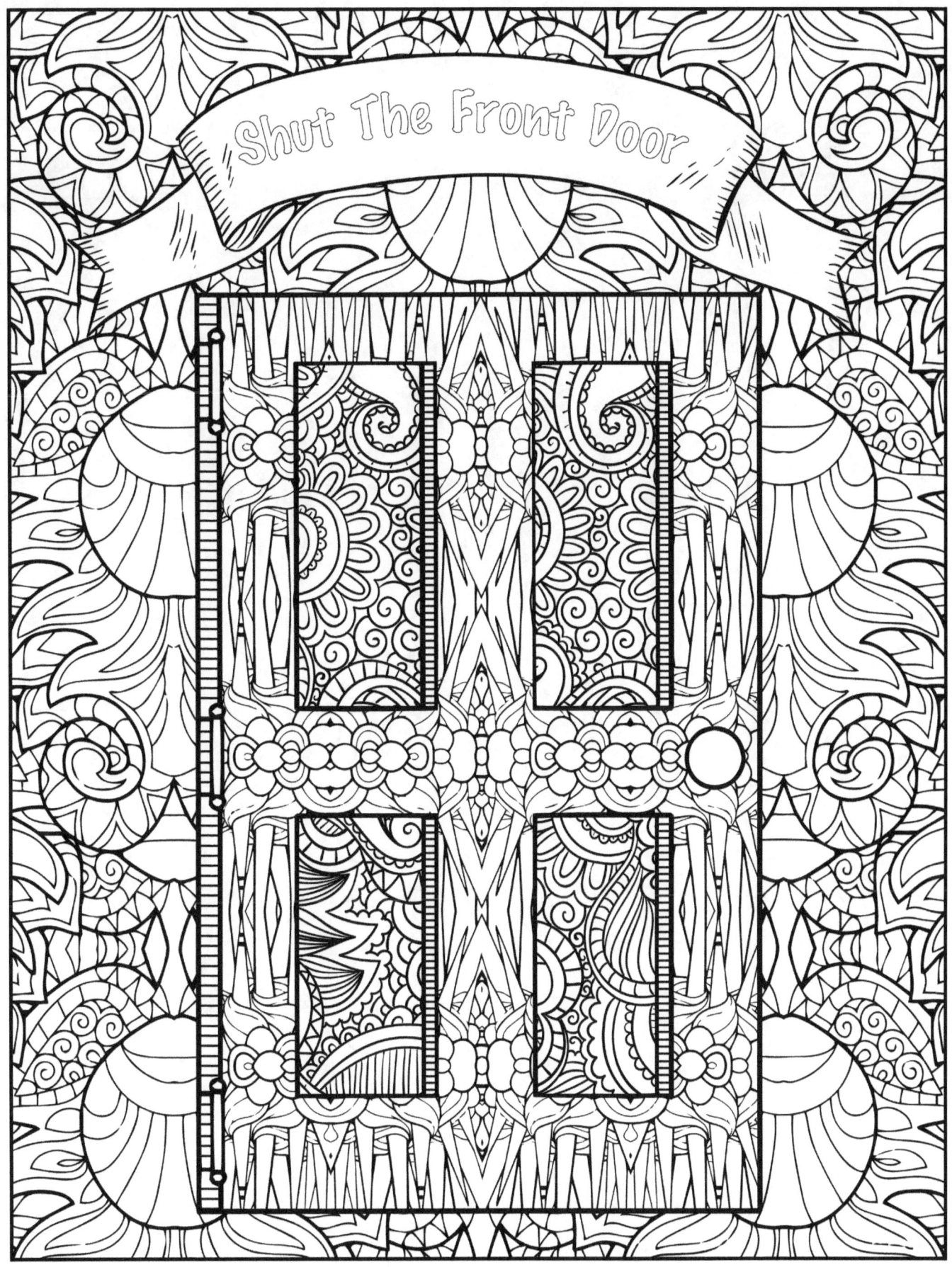

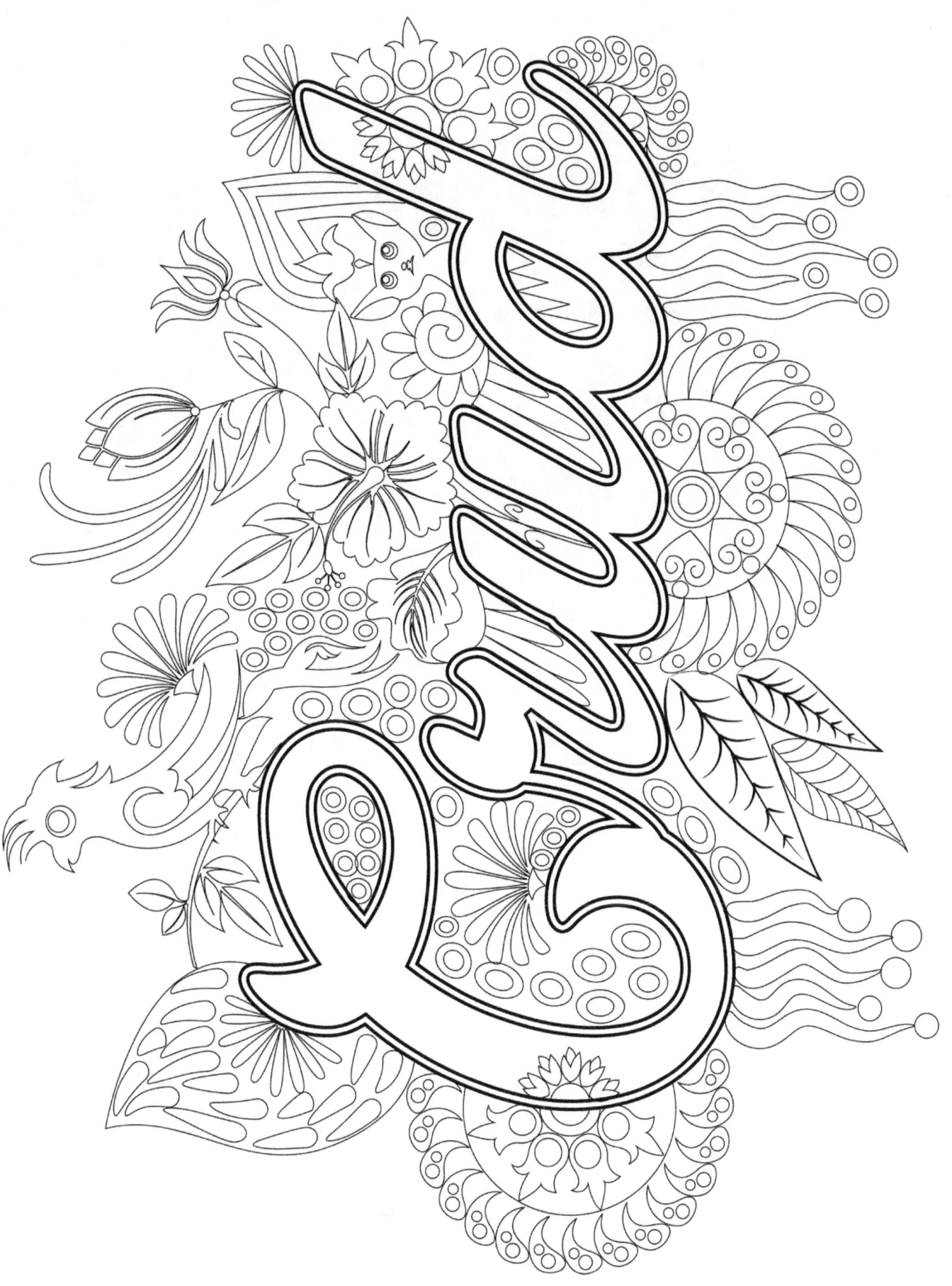

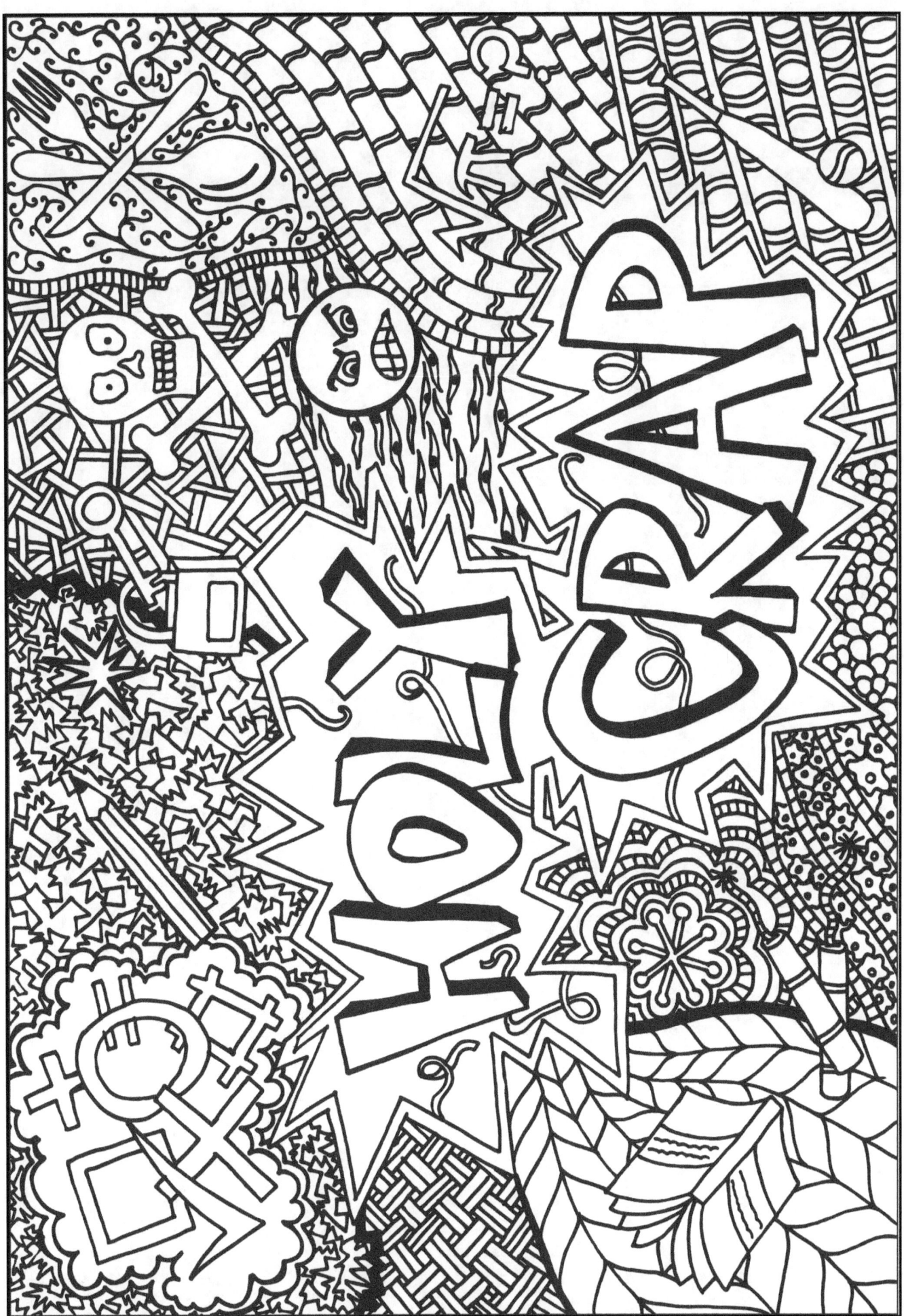

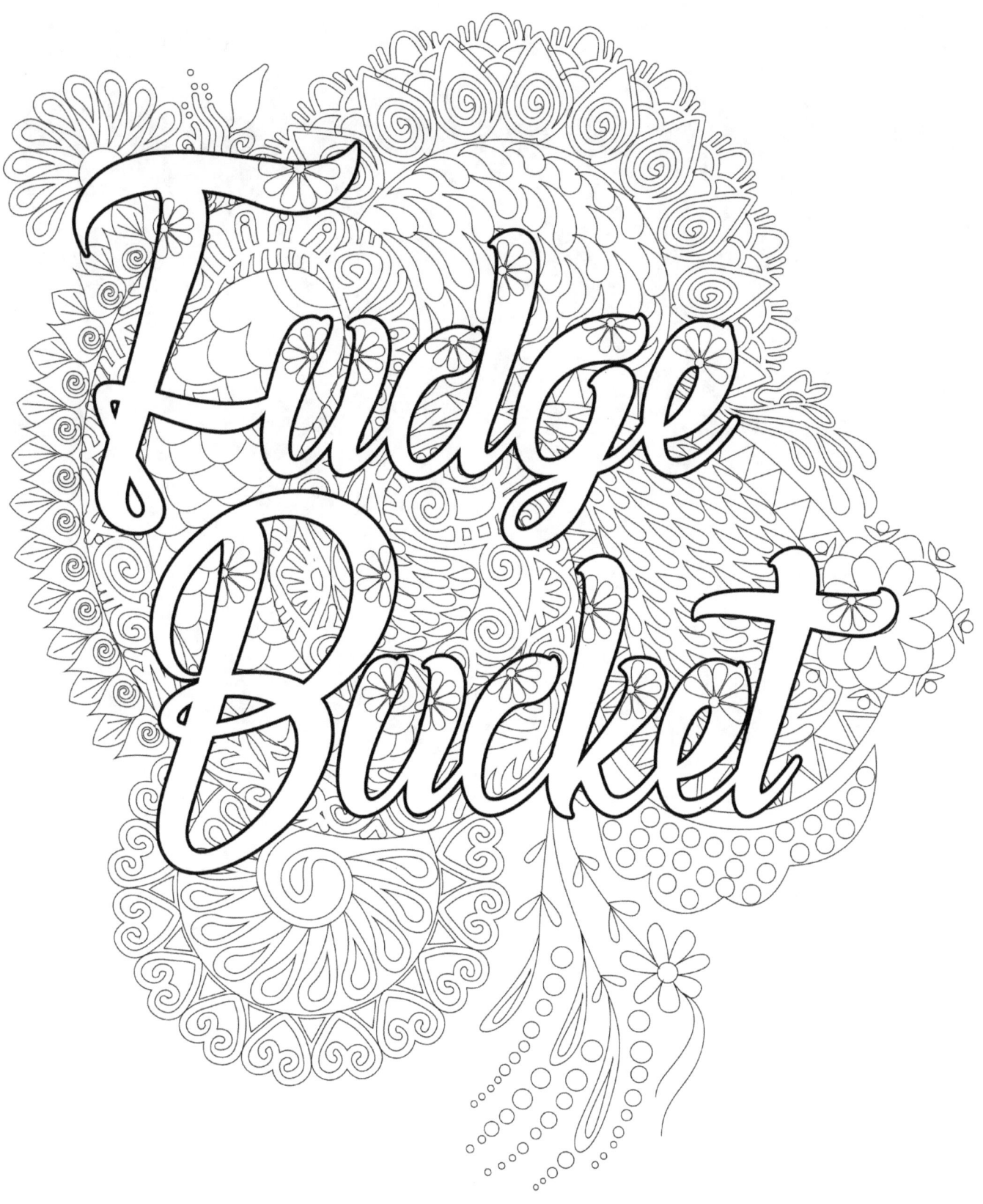

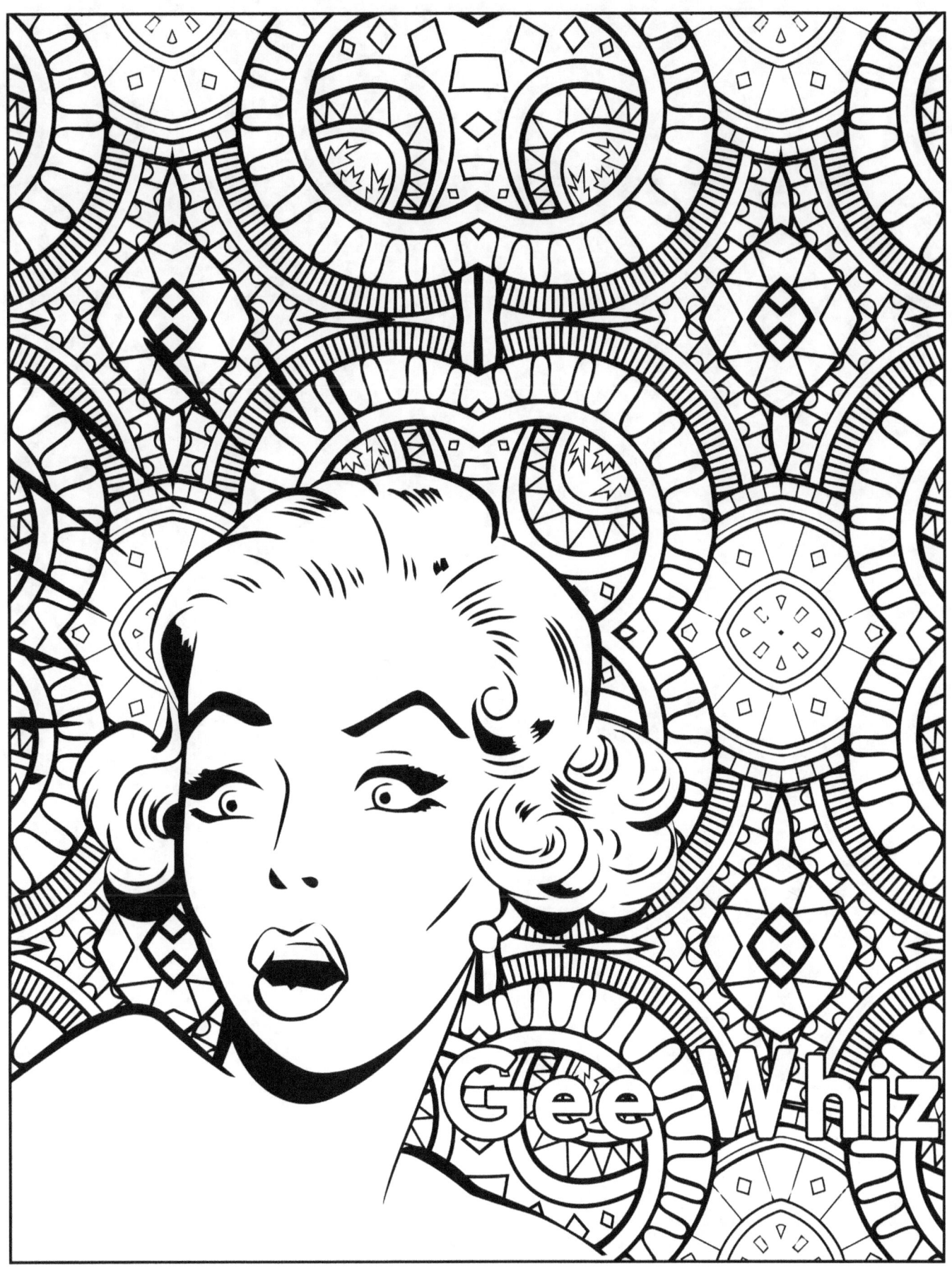

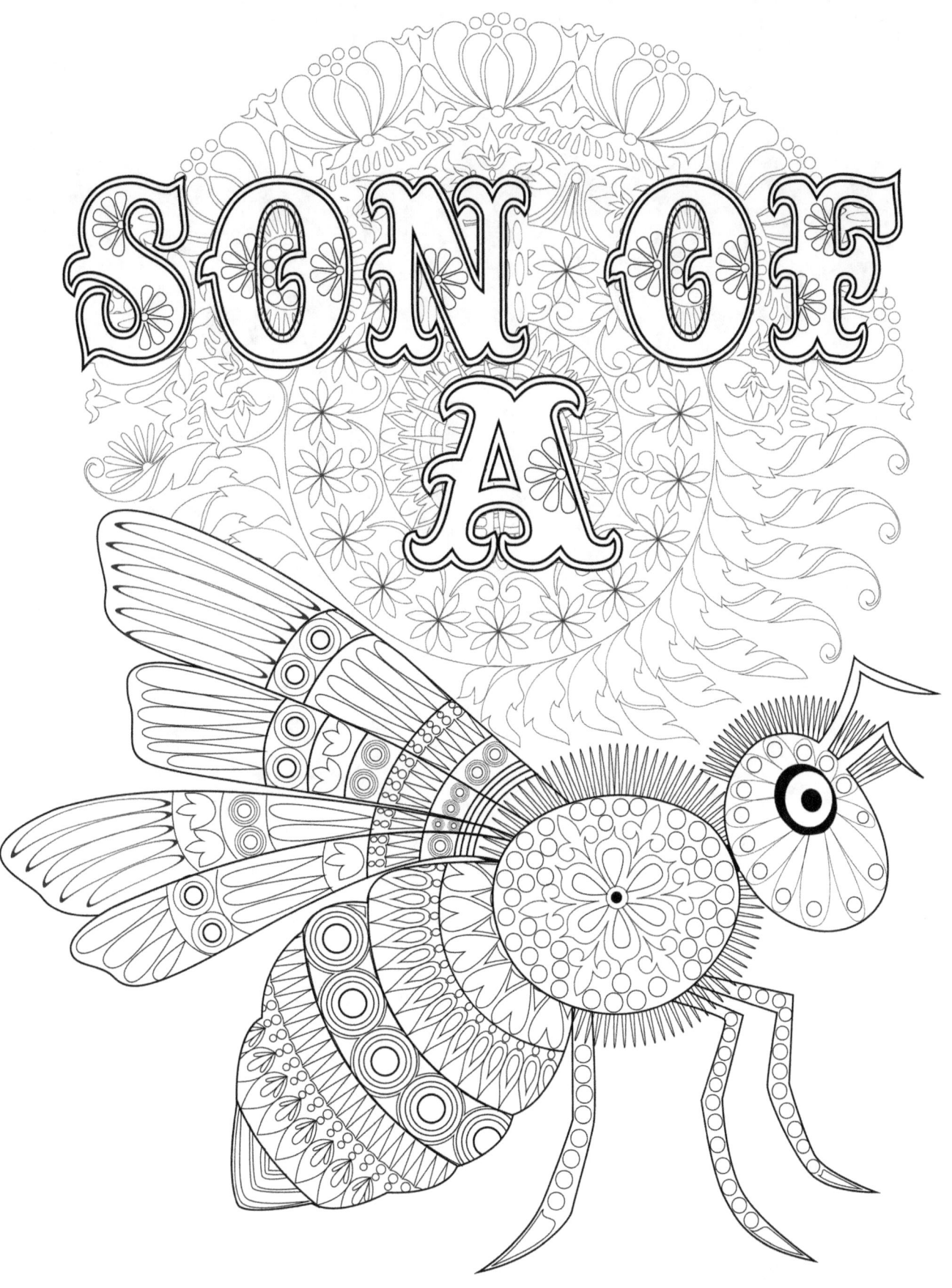

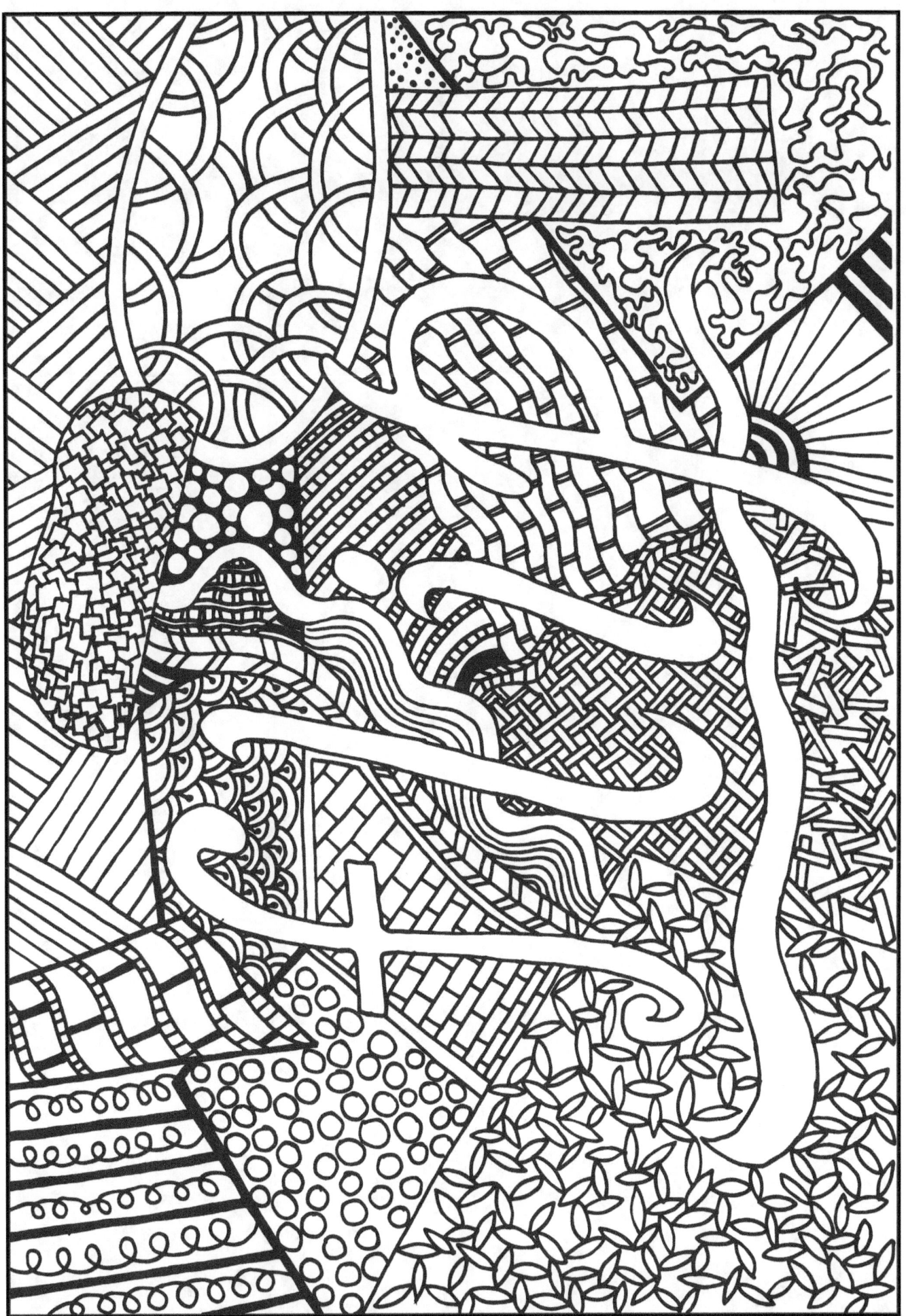

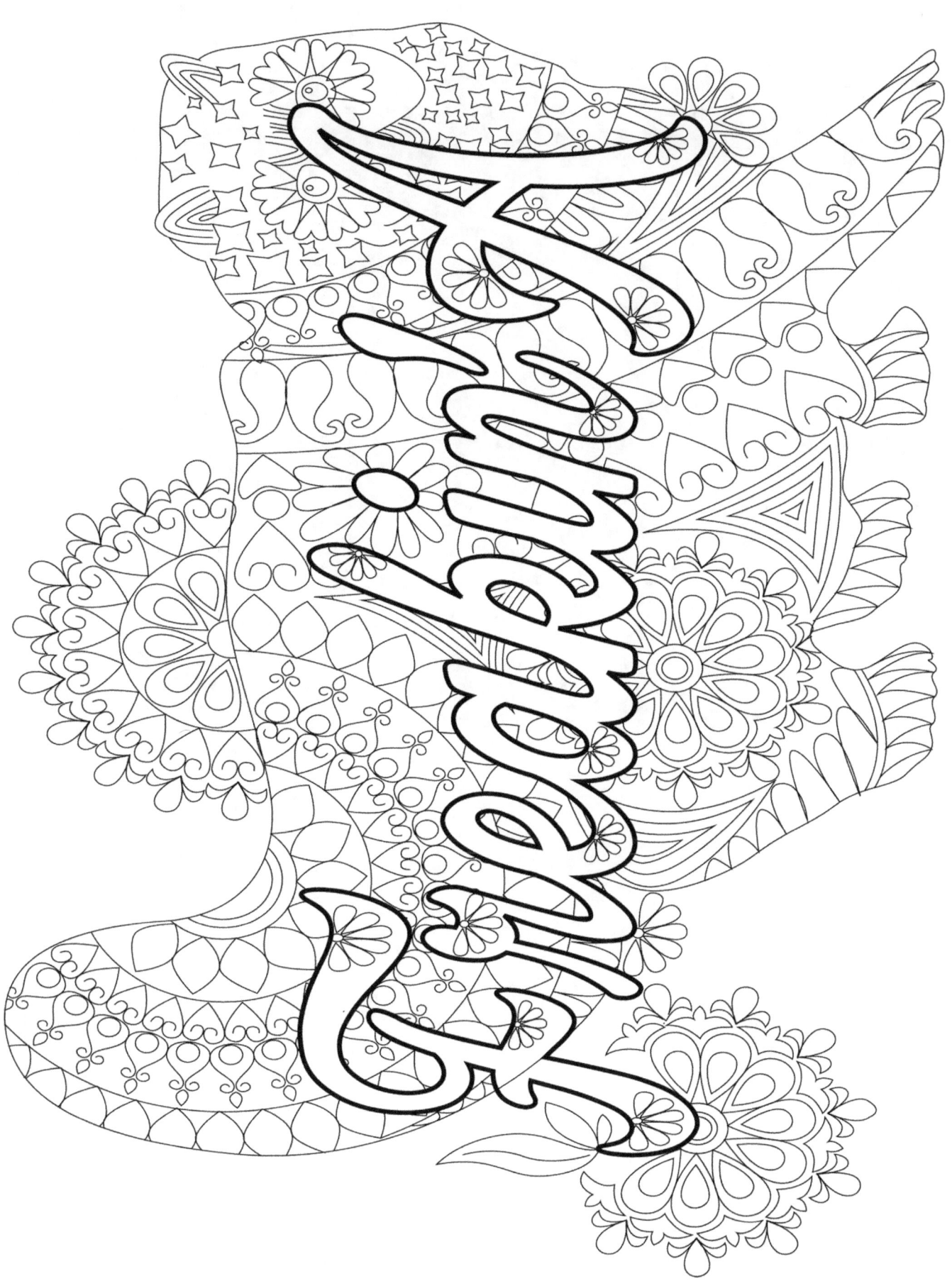

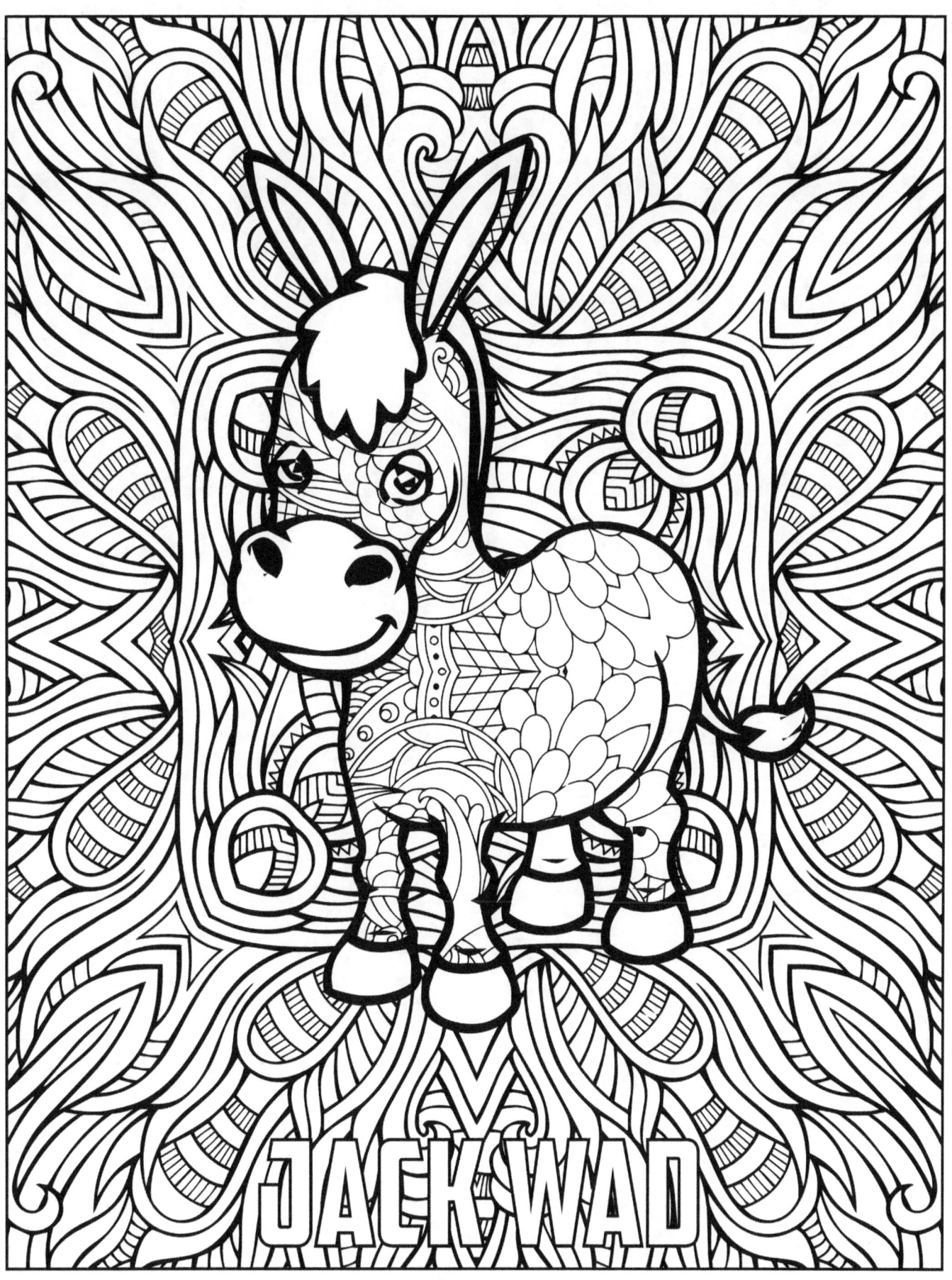

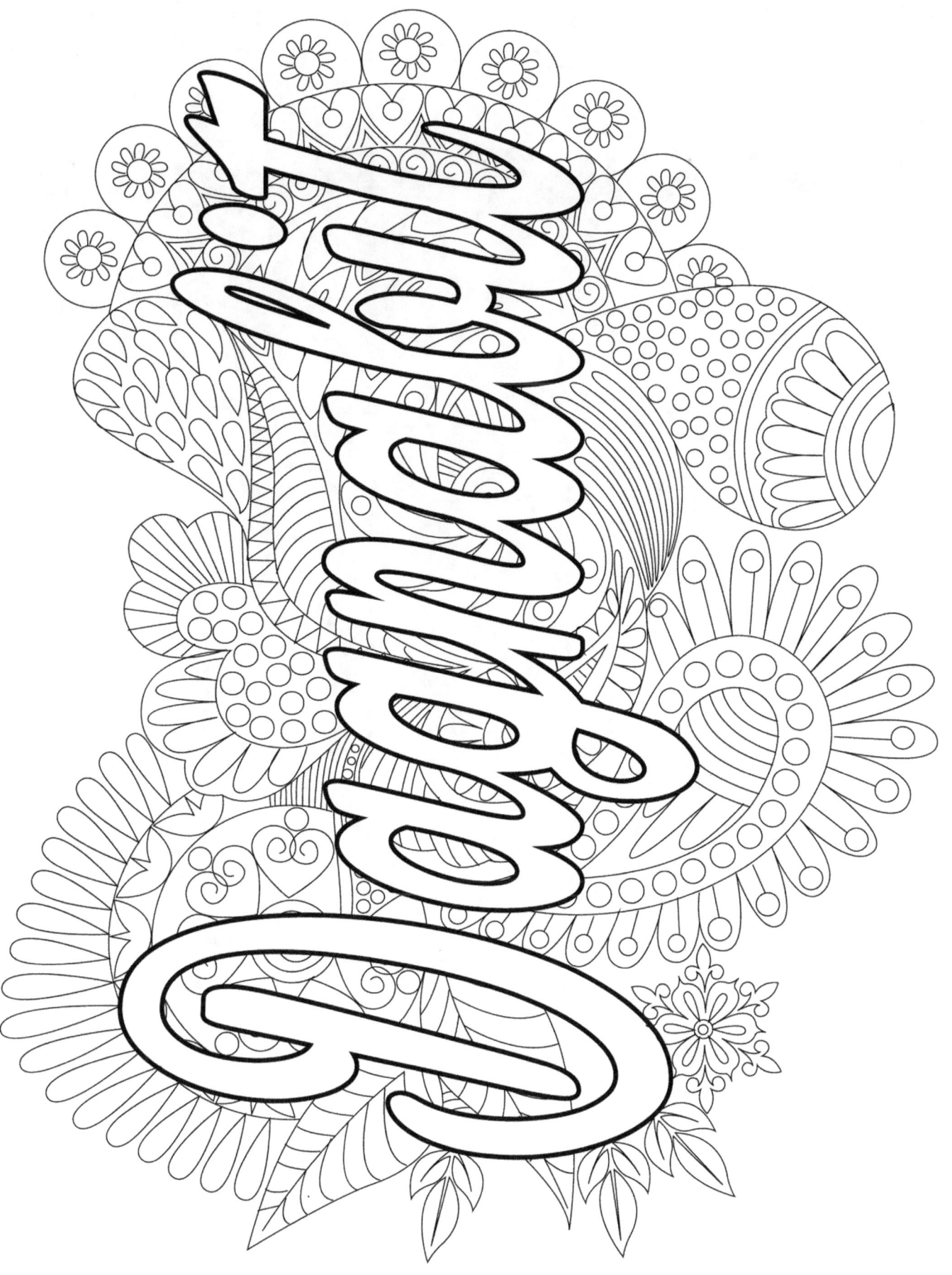

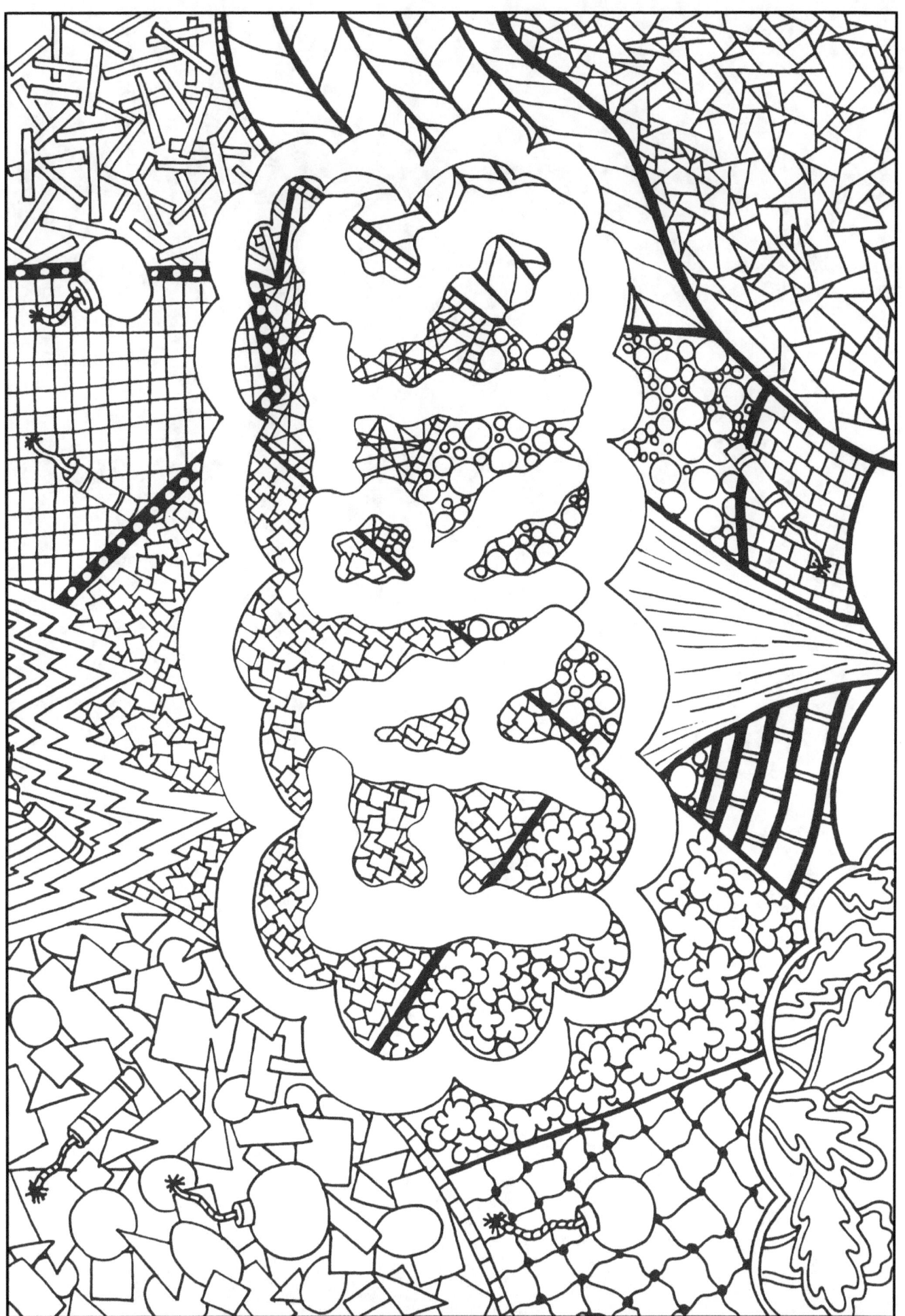

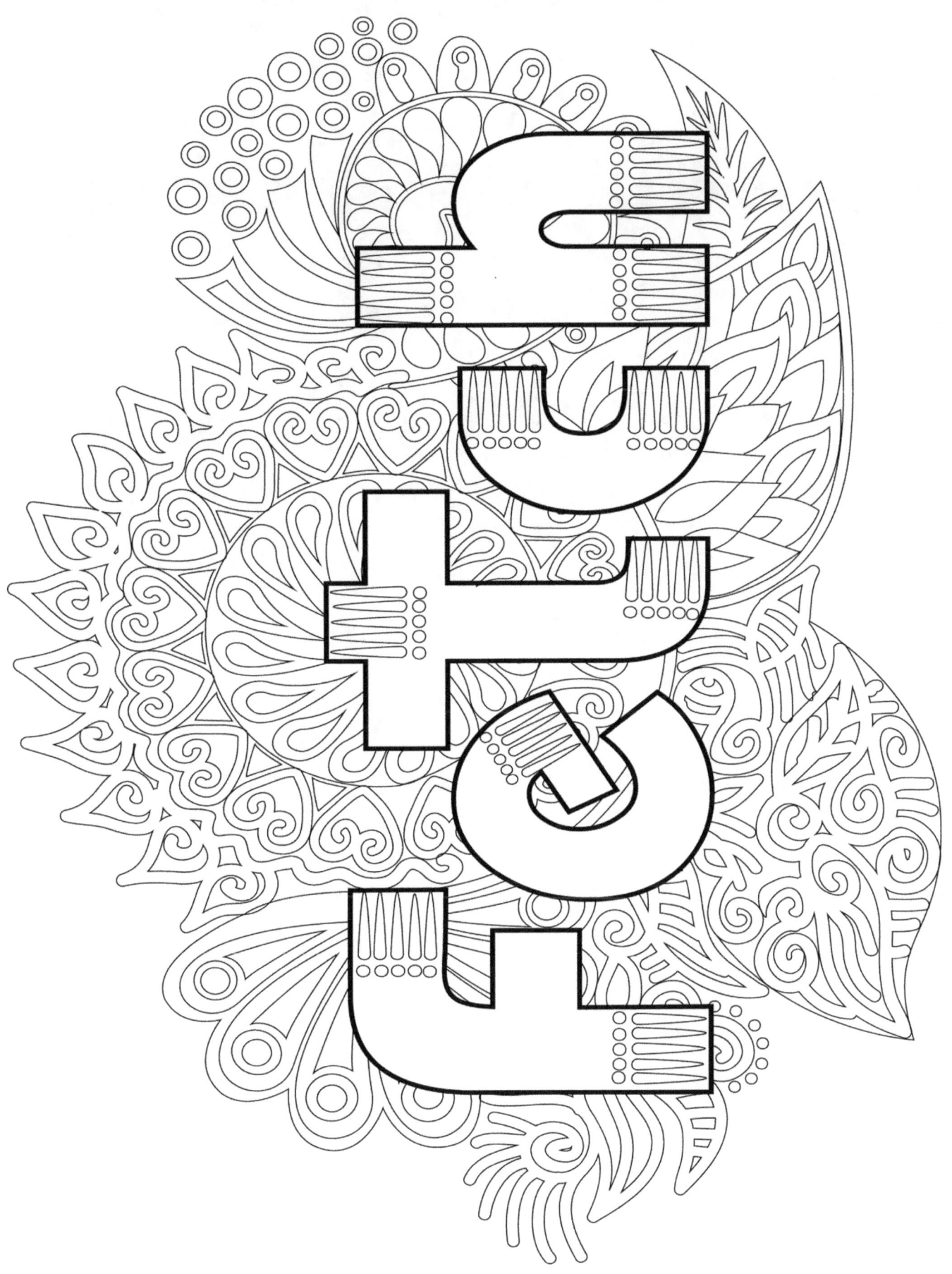

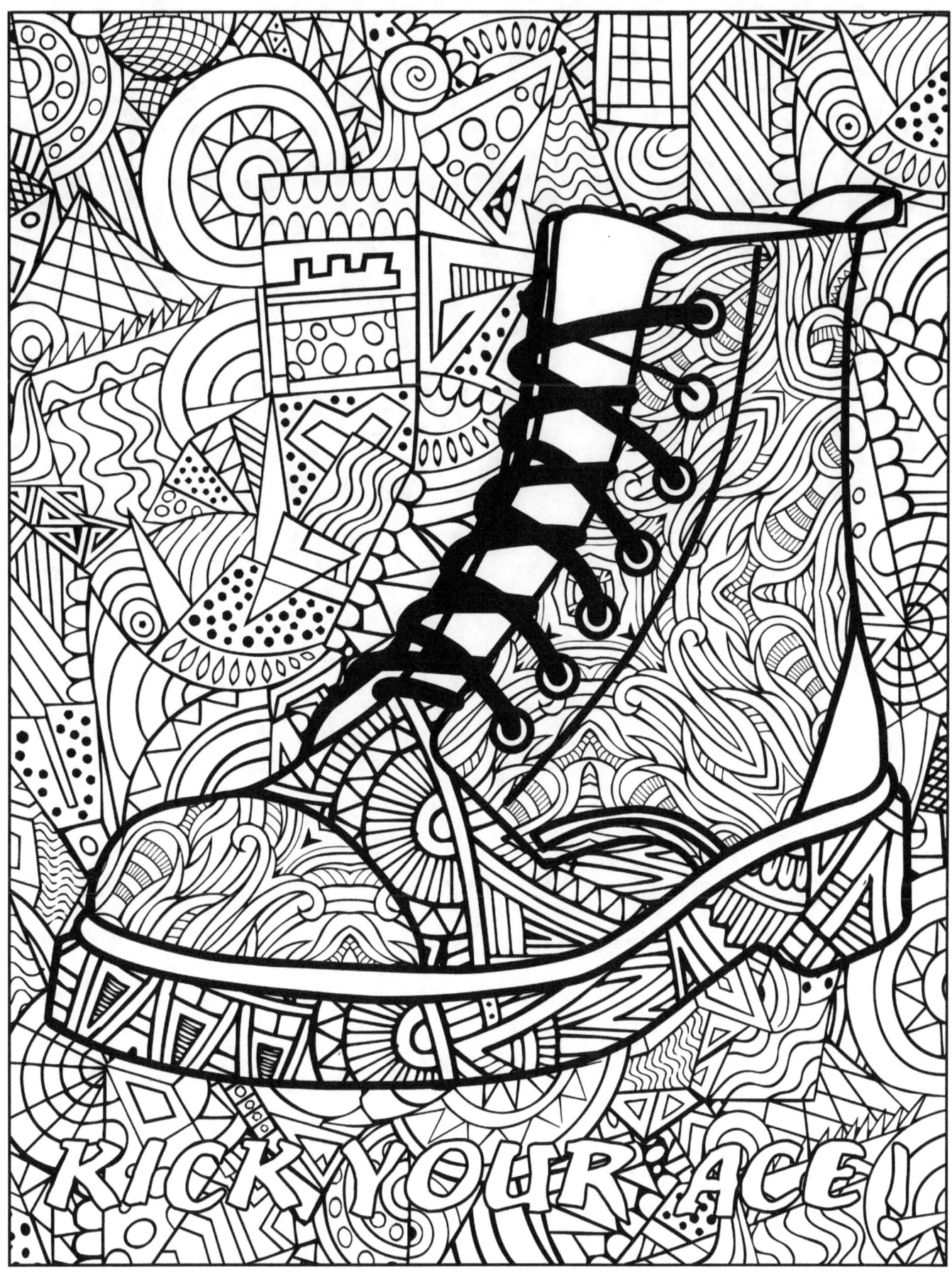

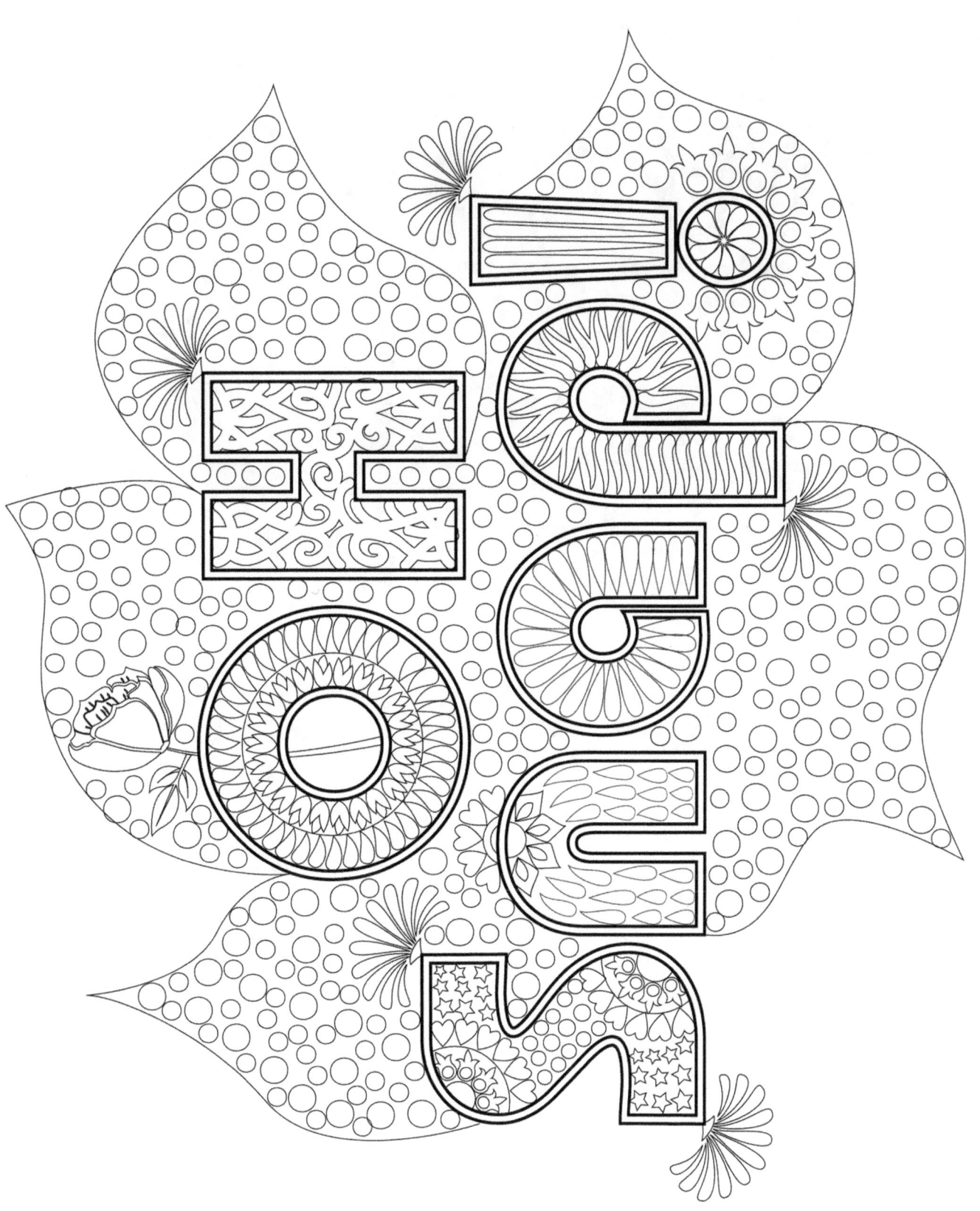

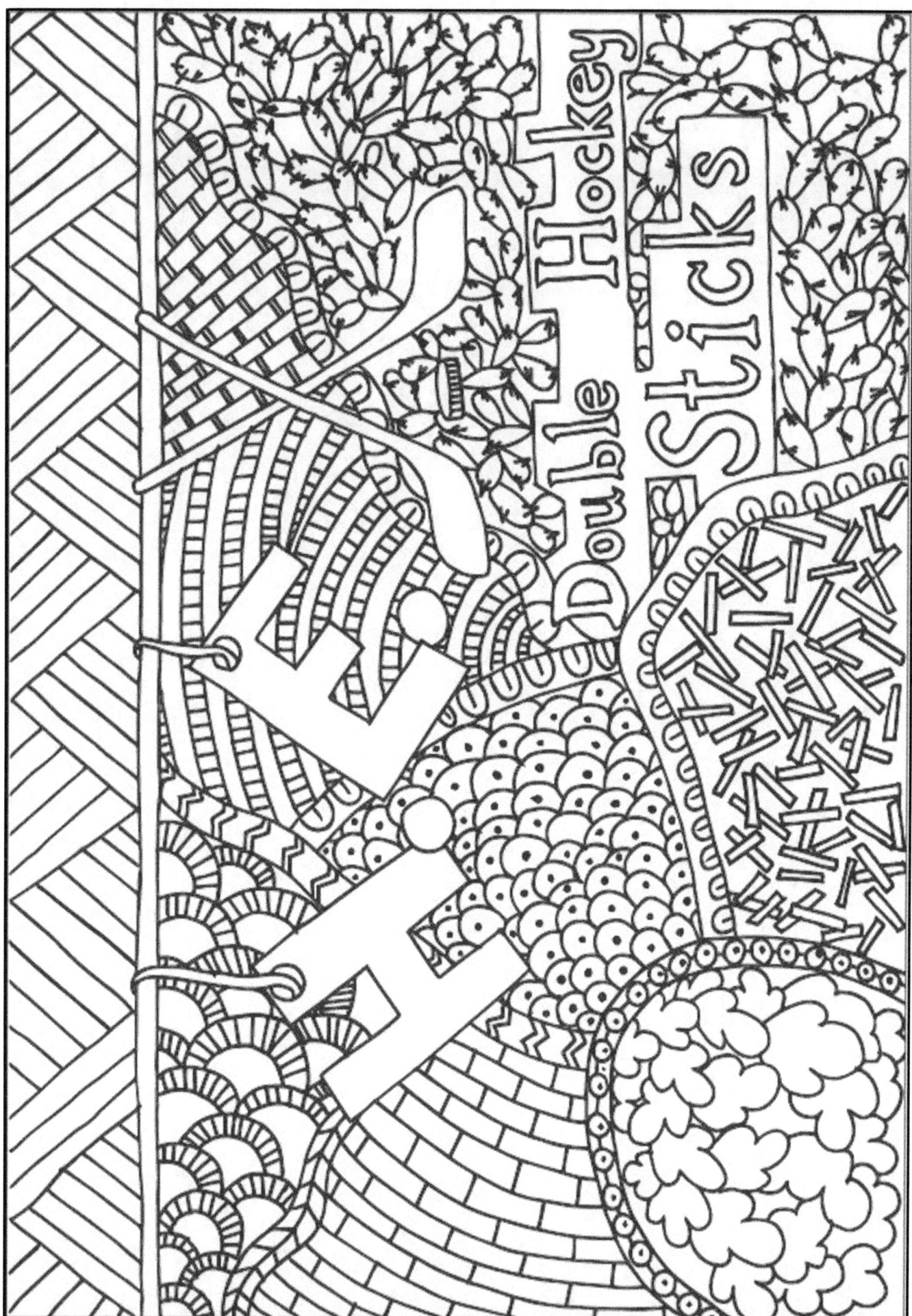

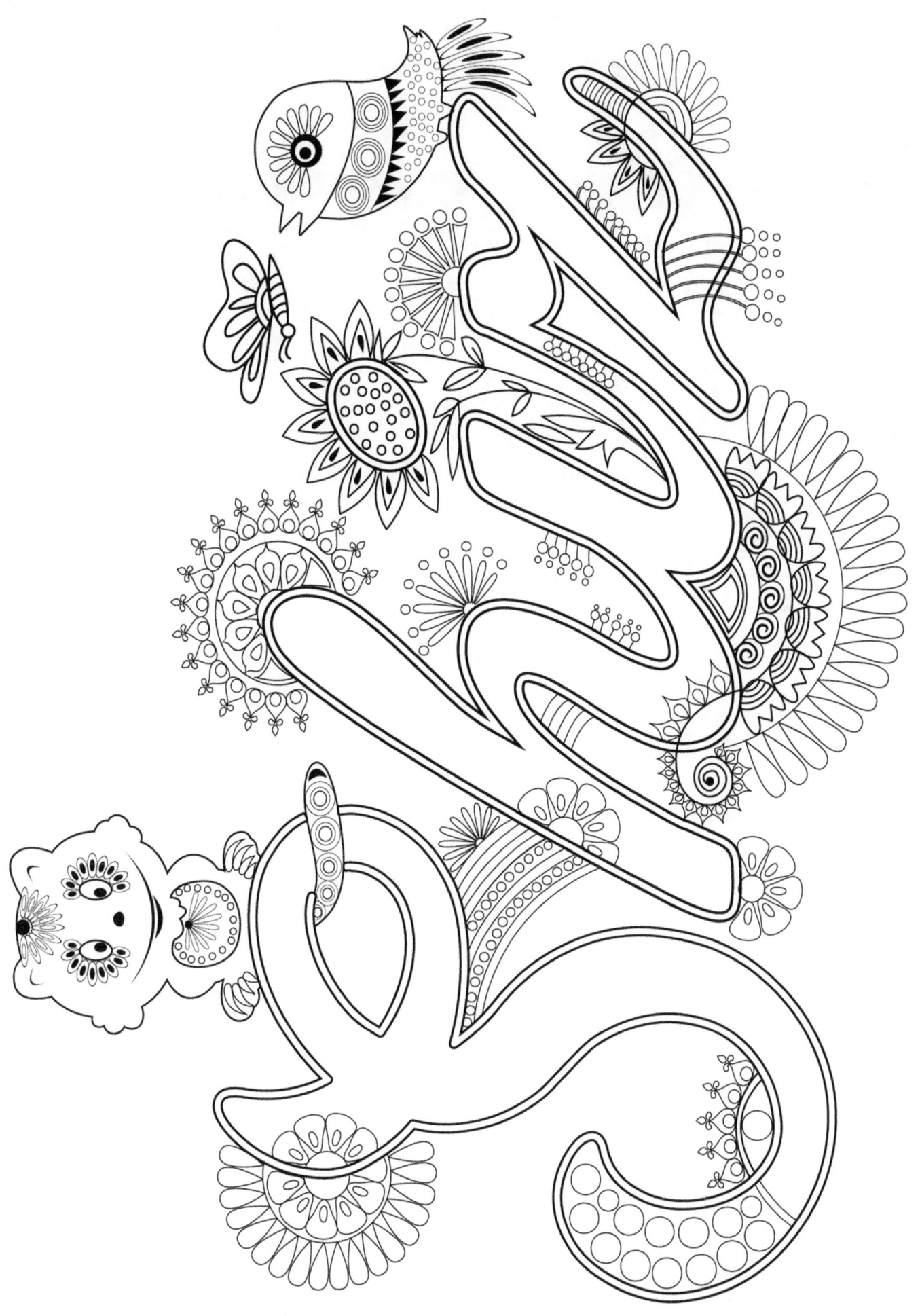

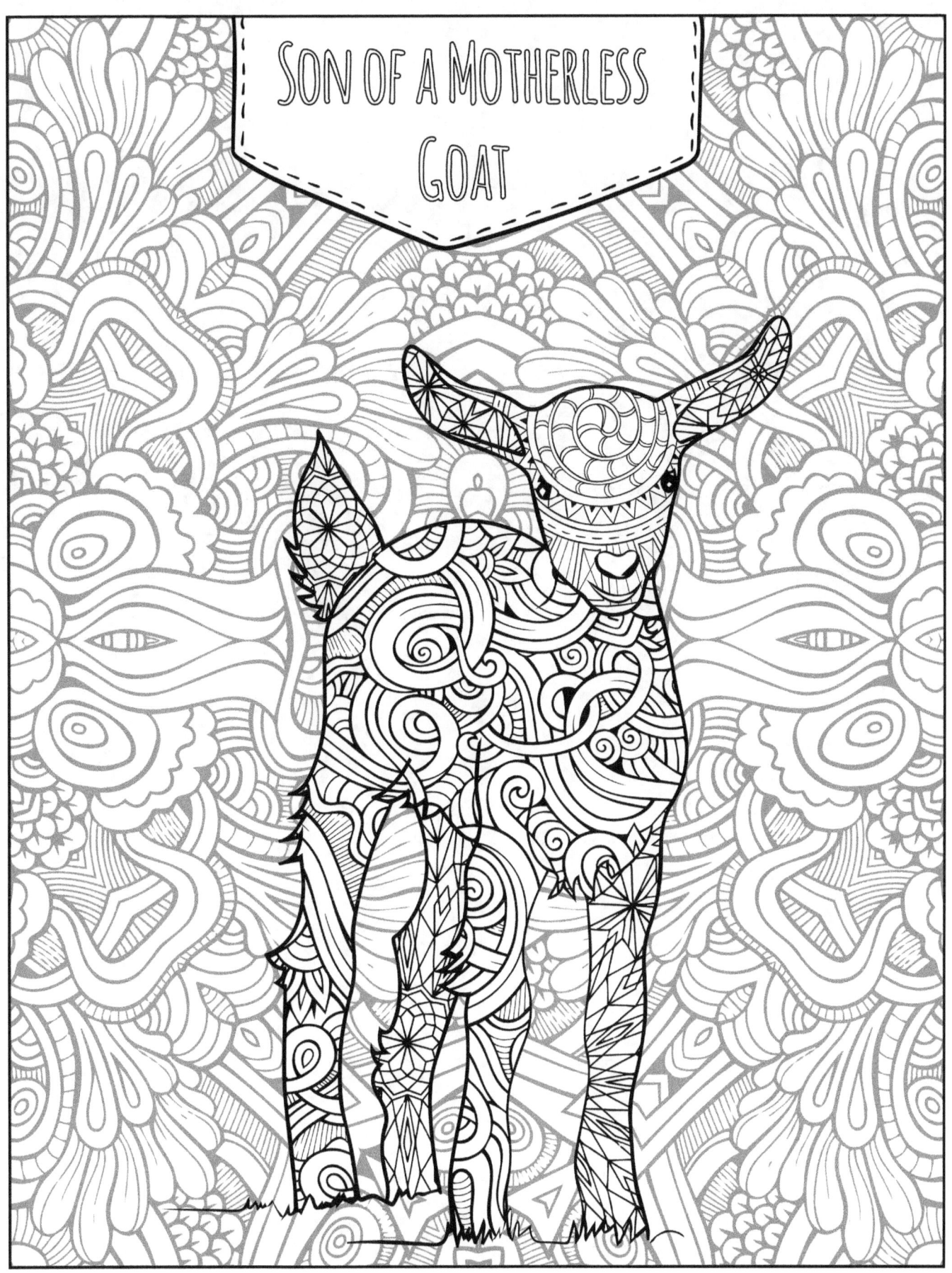

Son of a Motherless Goat

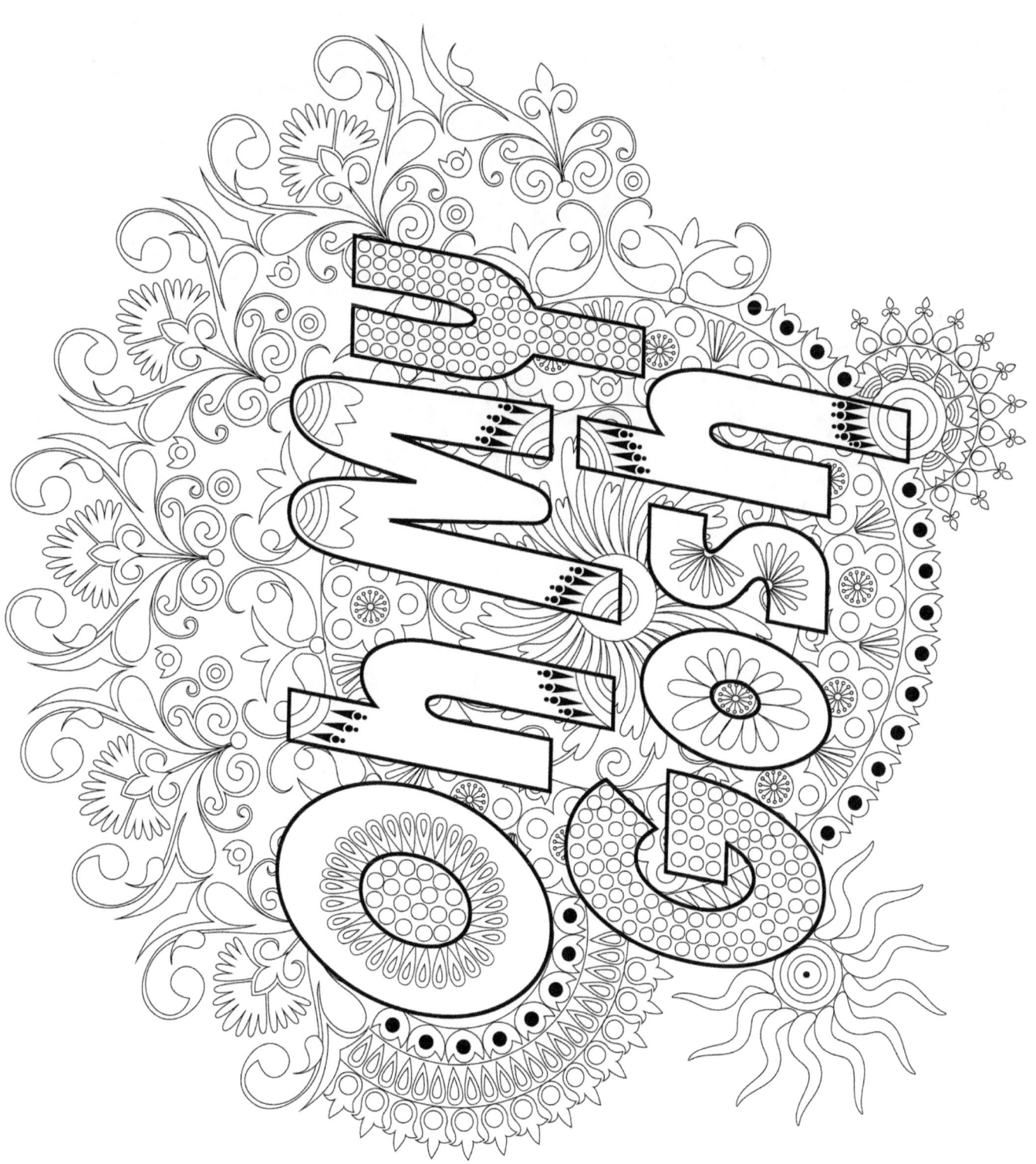

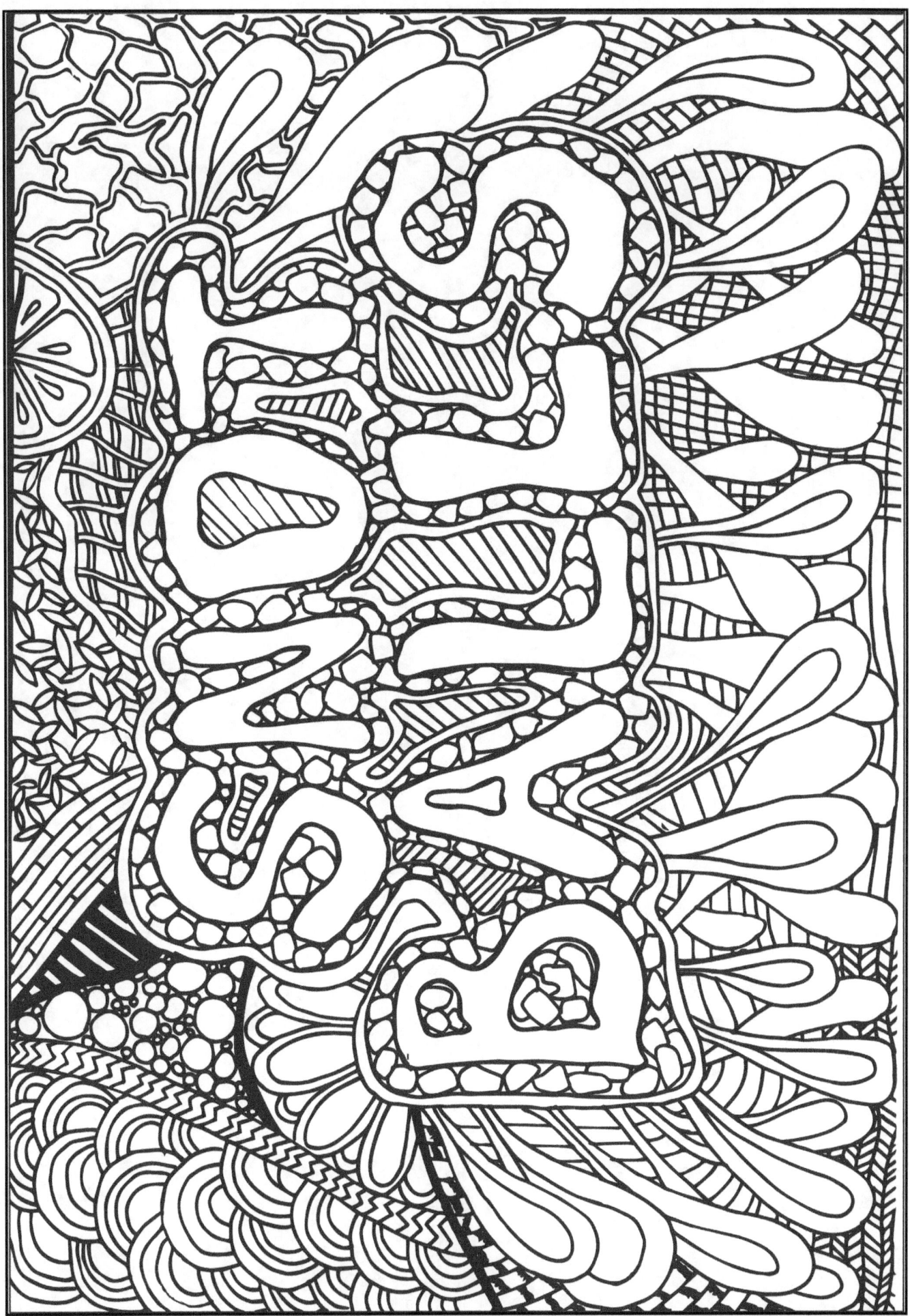

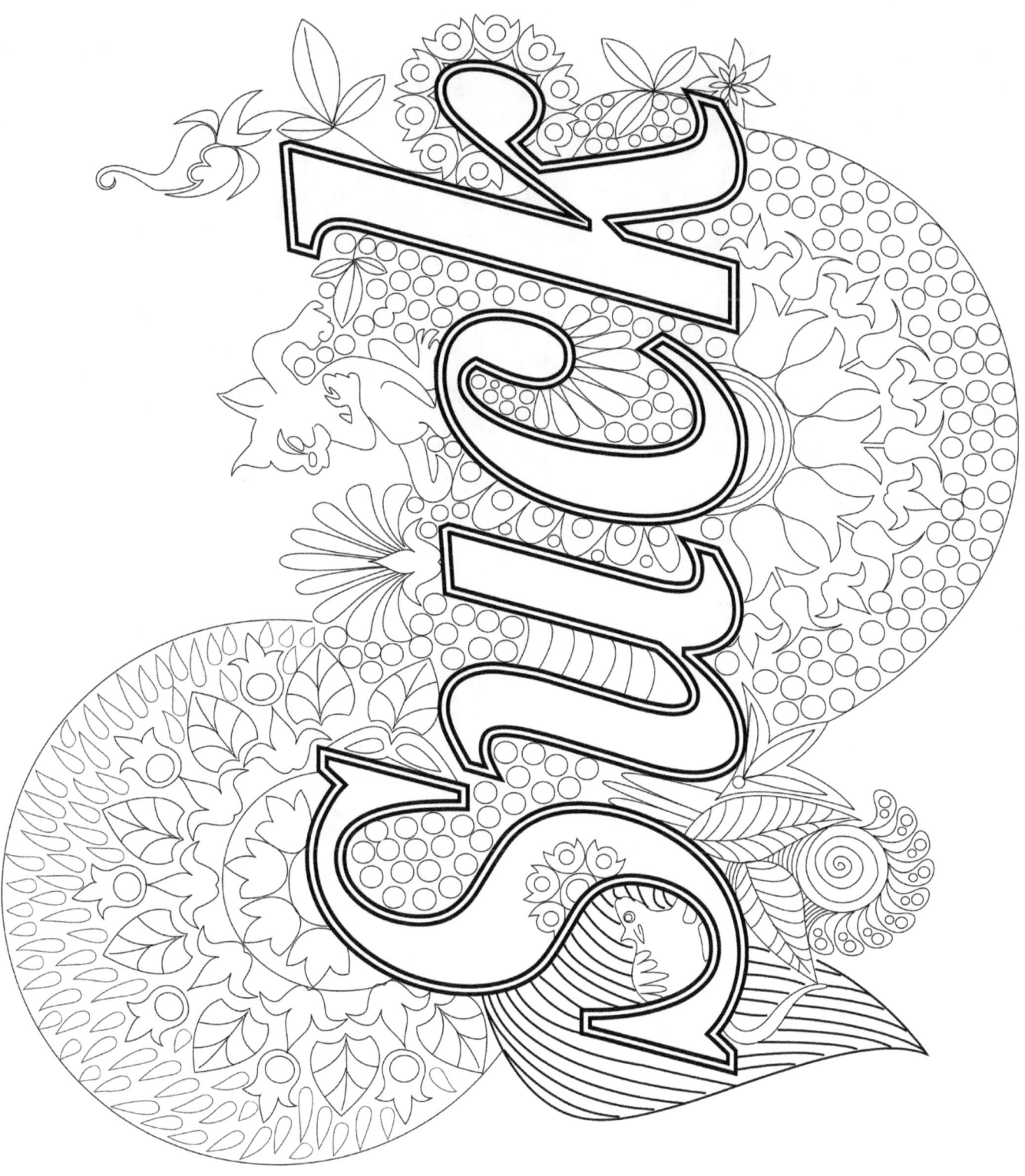

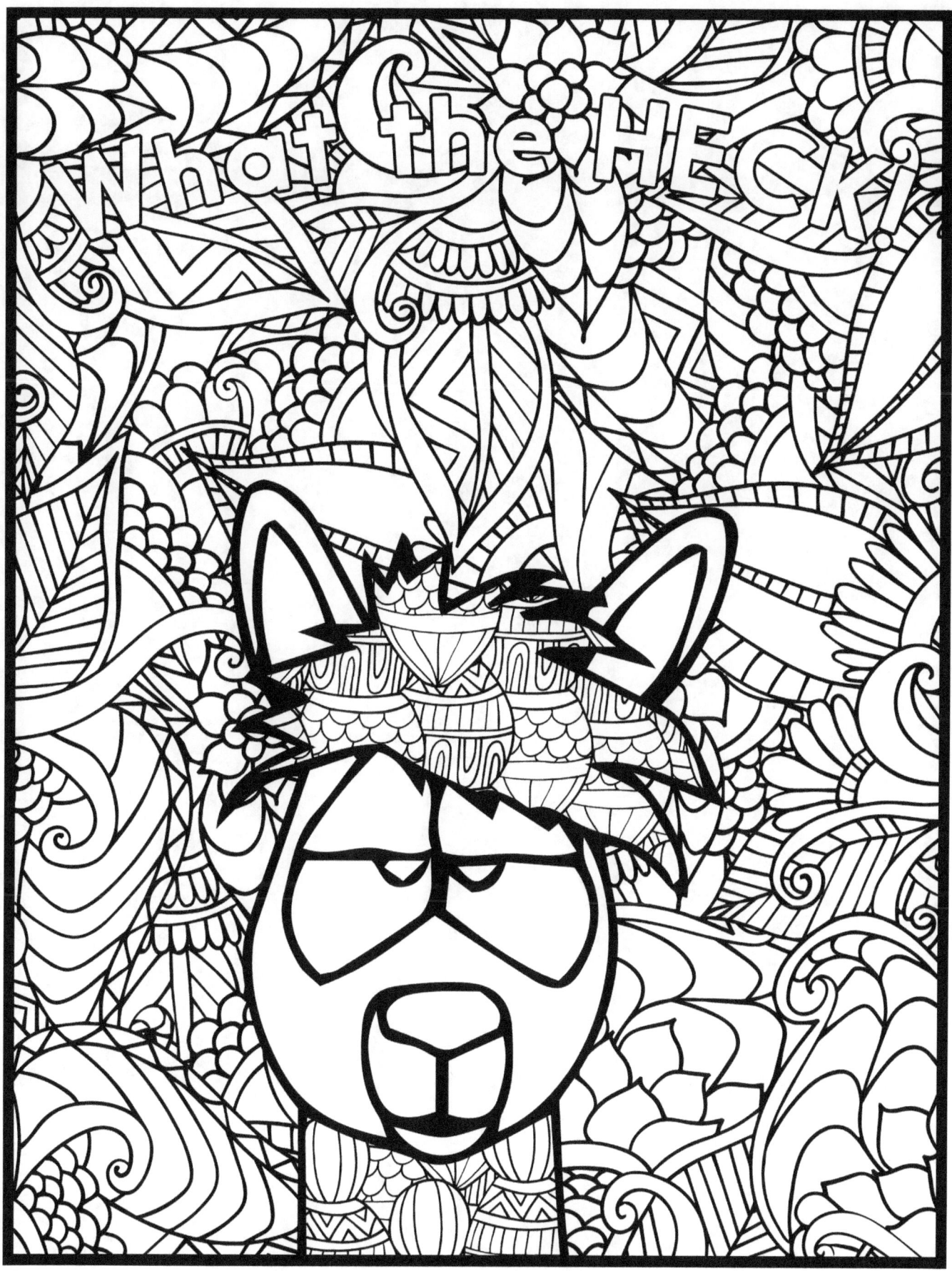

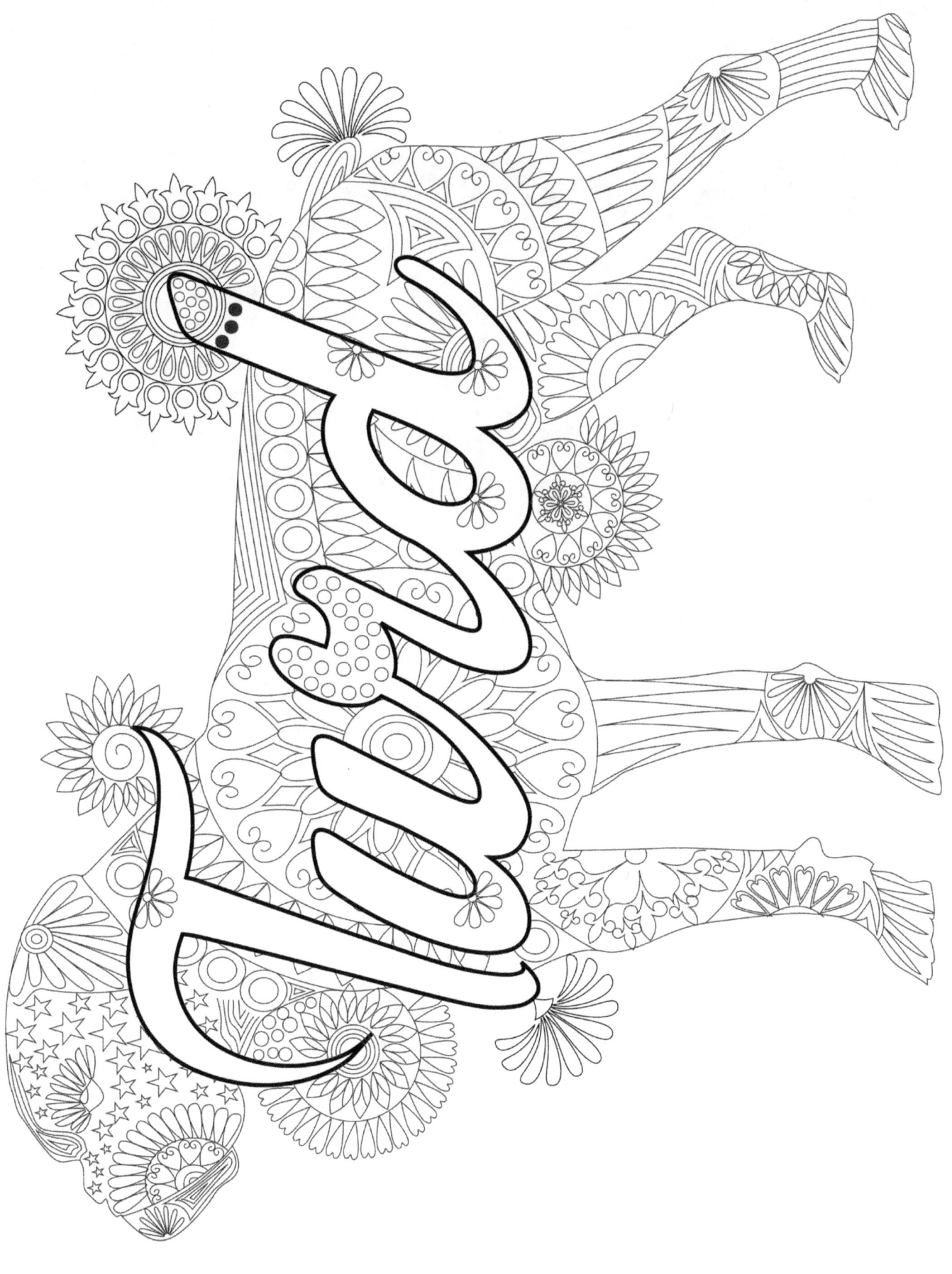

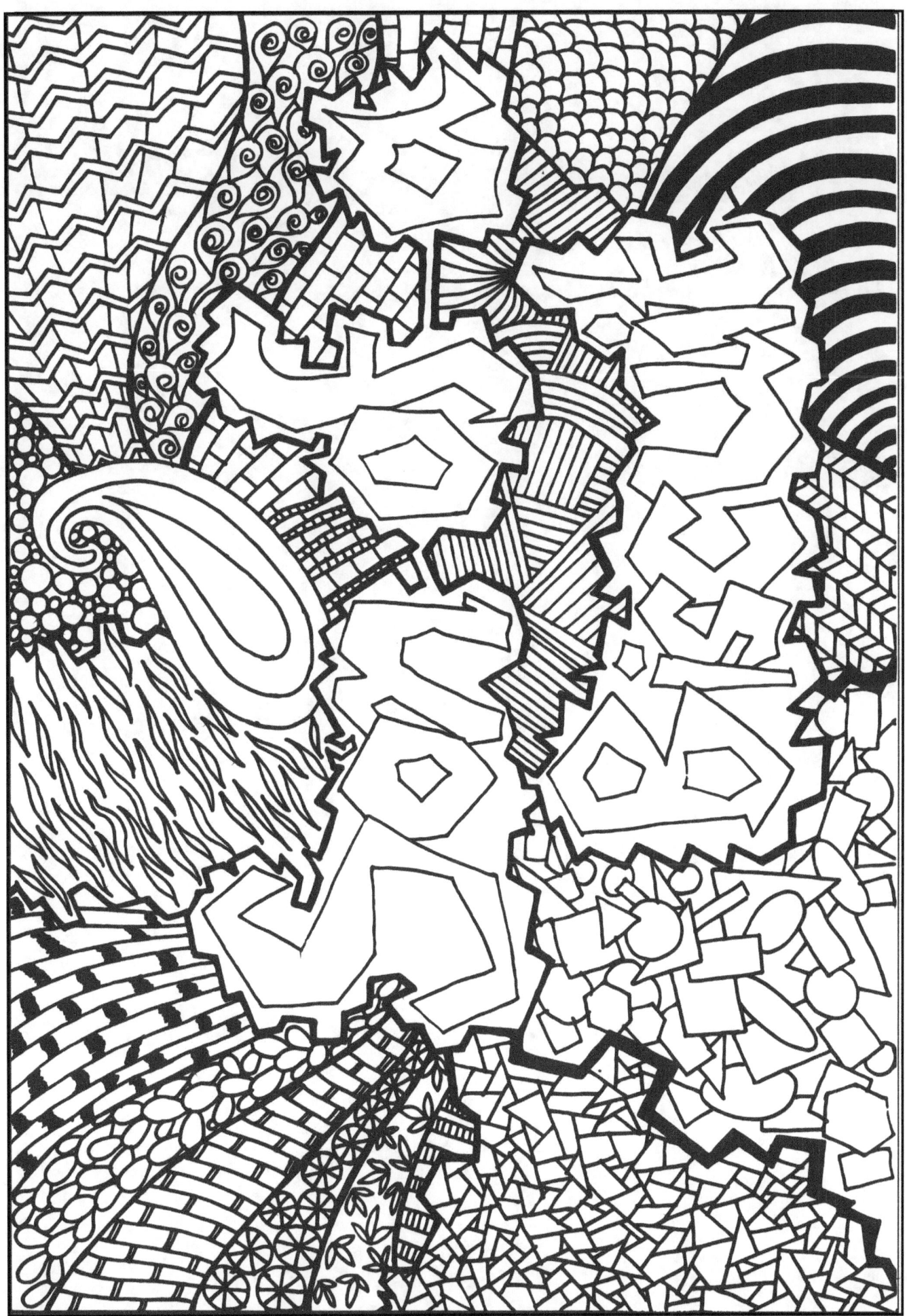

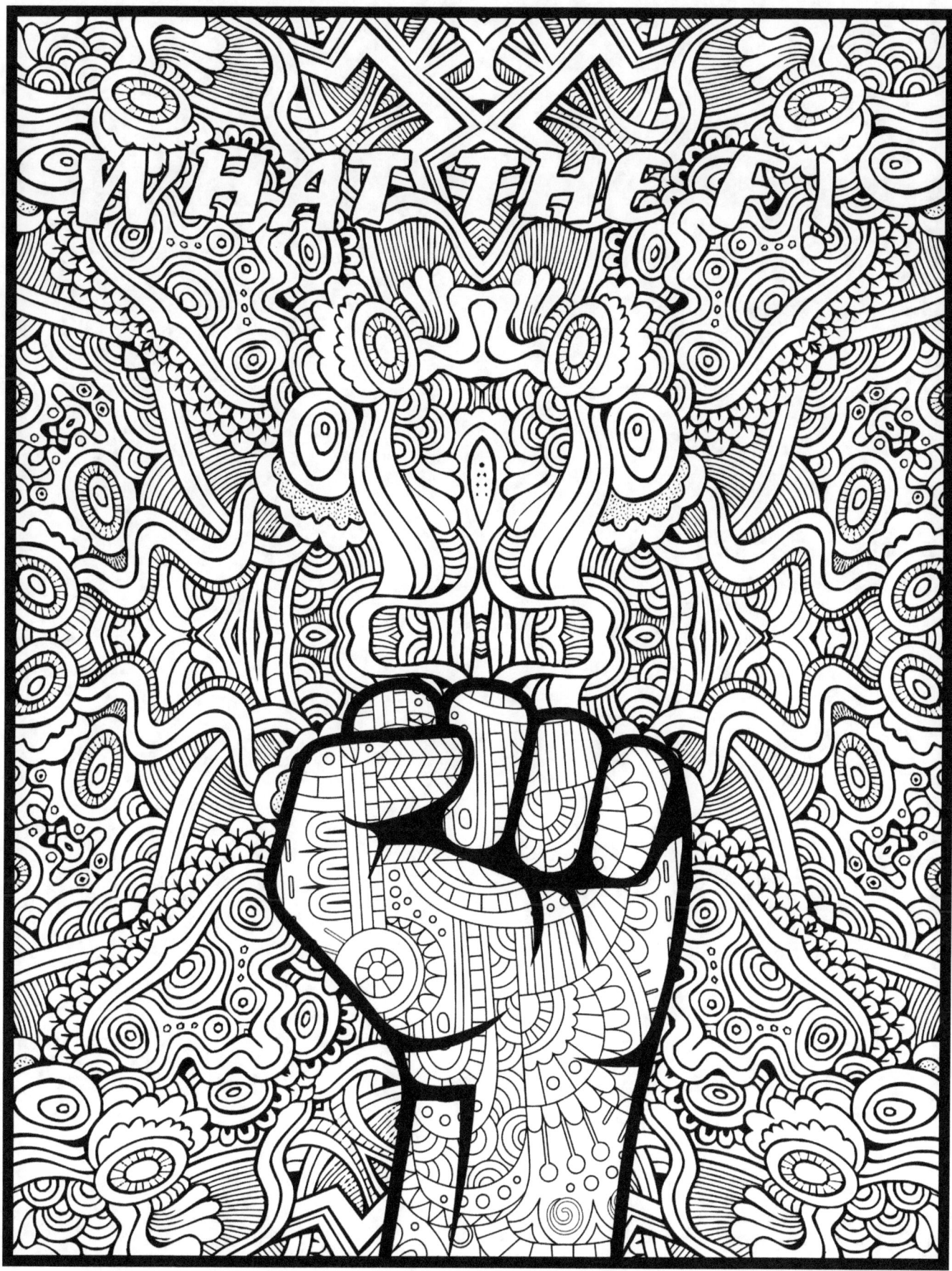

FIDDLESTICKS

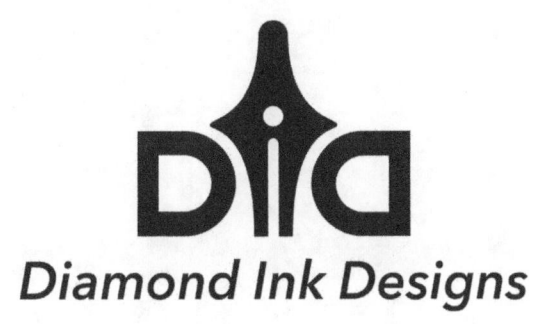

Diamond Ink Designs

Thank You

We hope you enjoyed our coloring book.
Please feel free to join our groups to be a part
of our future upcoming books and giveaways.

Visit and like us on Facebook:
I Love Coloring
www.facebook.com/HapyColoring

VIP CLUB:
http://eepurl.com/bQPz5f

Email:
did.color@gmail.com

www.ingramcontent.com/pod-product-compliance
Lightning Source LLC
Chambersburg PA
CBHW080550190526
45169CB00007B/2714